PILGRIMS OF SPACE

MUHAMED FARHAAN

WE DEDICATE THIS BOOK TO ALMIGHTY AND FAMILY
AND FRIENDS

Contents

Contents

Preface

"Space, it says, is big. Really big. You just won't believe how vastly, hugely, mindbogglingly big it is."

- Douglas Adams.

SO MUCH OF UNIVERSE TO BE EXPLORED, BUT TOO LESS TIME.

PILGRIMS OF SPACE IS AN ANTHOLOGY WHERE WE TAKE DEEP DIVE TO DISCOVER THE UNIVERSE AND BEYOND.

Acknowledgements

TO EVERYONE WHO SUPPORTED ME IN THIS PROJECT
THE BACK BONE:

Anuvab Dutta

Sydney Pierce

Awofisan Oluwadamilola Samson

Debra Sue Lynn

Daniel Duhaime

Jeff Cox

Essama Chiba

Himanshu Singla

Binod Dawadi

Amd.Maid Corbic

Jaspreet Kaur

Malavika Balasubramaniam

Melva Gifford

Mustafa Hakan çeliker

Pradnyesh Rajendra Ingole

Tisham Dhar

Smriti Pai

Joyce Lancaster

A B Preethika

Sai Sravanthi

Nivedha V

Rashmi Bajpai

ACKNOWLEDGEMENTS

Sujatha.R

Shakil Kalam

Shakil Ahmed

Abdulloh Abdumominov

Afrah Sadiqa S S

Nivedha SS

Bhavya M Bhaskaran

Andrew Fort

Neelam Lashari

Javeria Aziz

1. Passenger from Earth

Away from fake love and hate,
Not willing to reincarnate.
I fly into the silence of space,
Where there is no discrimination from caste and race,
Here no one falls for a face.
No nonsense ideology,
Only driven by cosmic energy
I slide by the rings of Saturn
No plans of a u turn,
No body shaming
No one calls here, Jupiter obese
I play hide and seek with the moons of Mars,
A beautiful life in between stars.
The Earth gave us so much
But we misused it's land,
I won't let anyone pollute the milky way band.
I wish I could live here forever.
Watch the day and night in turns take birth,
Sadly, I am just a passenger from earth.

2. Galaxy Express

A single soul
In a new over haul
Off through the black hole
Born to express,
Not to impress
On the galaxy express
Falling stars are like flakes of snow
Earth is the only one with life I know
Life is the only boat I row
Travel miles way in light years
Telling tales from where I come
Born to express
Not to impress
On the galaxy express
I spell out the truth
Yes each human has been assigned by almighty for a role to play
Yes there still discrimination here against lesbian and gay
Yes we still here lick oreo.
Still on the process to break tapes that are stereo.
Born to express
Not to impress
On the galaxy express

MUHAMED FARHAAN

World is a family
Our race descended from the garden of Eden,
Universe still has gems that are hidden.
In the quest
On the galaxy express
Born to express
Not to impress

3. When I met you on Mars

In a quest to explore,
I soar.
Finally, I stepped on a planet,
Red, as a fresh pomegranate.
In search of life,
In search of love,
Not lust,
I walk on the Star dust.
A homosapien in a space suit,
Trying to find a route.
Found you in a crater beside the Olympus mons hills,
Absolutely chills.
Two lives meet,
Promised to be loyal,
Knowing both do not belong to the same soil.
Love is in the air ,I say
Under the Phobos and Deimos we stay
Two lives in the galaxy - milky way.
Life changed when I met you on mars,
We are a pair made in stars.

Now I have somebody at my worse,
Amidst of zillions of stars, this is the glory of universe.

4. When I met you on Mars 2.0

Martian surface appears dry
My eyes get heavy,
And I cry
In solitude i lie
Why did I come here
Why
My days on earth are gone,
Didn't have bonds there like nylon
But Mars has no gardens like Babylon
Had an earthquake in my rib cage
Nothing but fluttering butterflies,
When I met your eyes.
Promised our relationship won't be build on lies.
Asked whether you will be my valentine
Even though I come from the land of Einstein
With a different sun sign.
Titan in Eclipse,
Today in bliss
With extreme breeze
Mars is cooler than earth

MUHAMED FARHAAN

I'm freeze
Lets capture this memory in a photograph
Lets say cheese.
This a planet where there is no caste no bars
Life changed when I met you on Mars.

5. Only Earth is worth

I went to the sun
But embrace it's warmth
But got burnt
I went to the farthest corner of the milky way
To make my hot head ego feel cooler
But got frozen
I went to the Saturn
The one with the ring
Looking angelic
But turned out be circle of stone faced , rusted rocks
I went to Mars , took seek some divine red dust.
But it was only my lust
Went to the Jupiter , to play with its moons,
It it turned out to be a goon.
Nor mercury, Venus, neither Uranus and Neptune
Only Earth
That's worth

6. Saturn

Saturn
In the galaxy, a beautiful lantern
An angelic ring
A friend like Titan
Some consider it bad luck
I went embrace it's coolness
But got frozen
It's a gas giant
Obviously not a noble saint

About the Compiler

Dr.Muhamed Farhaan is currently doing his internship in dentistry in Thai Moogambigai Dental college and hospital, DR MGR UNIVERSITY, Chennai. He completed his schooling from MES RAZEENA MHSS, CHENNAI and IIPS, RIYADH,KSA.He also holds a diploma in modern applied psychology from ACHOLOGY. He is also pursuing sports dentistry from IIST, Pune.He is has compiled 7 anthologies and 1 solo book. He has also been published as a co-author in 14 anthologies.He has collection of writeups of over 100 on instagram[@anonymoussoul23].

7. One-Way Ticket

One-way ticket, I sweared to my life
My dream made others think I am naive
One-way ticket, I kept looking up the sky -
Raising my hand, the space didn't seem too high
But now that I am on my mark,
I see the space as an infinite dark
Our spaceship has had quite a hazard
But this One-way Ticket made my limits surpassed.
Time after time, this infinite void
Showed stunning creations which we enjoyed
But the old phrase plays an important role -
"Behind a diamond, hides a lump of coal"
Those beautiful sights were meant to deceive
At the end, only battling did we receive
But now that I'm journeying, there's no retreat
I'll travel as far the space goes; my life's my ticket.
"Oh! Look Look! It's a nebula", exclaimed my mate
To the windows everyone made a haste
Sparkling radiants with vibrant hue,
Bluish glow among the dusty dew
Then out of nowhere, a battle arrived -
Thosands of fire balls left no place to hide

Our ship got struck hard, we heard the red beep
We had to gamble without thinking, taking a faith o' leap -
Engines started, machine rolled,
We travelled like a little mole
Dodging and up high, and down again from top
Getting into the fiery rain, no time to stop
Fast! Fast! Rushing through with speed
The gambling we took is one-way's deed
Getting through the fire balls, we saw the enemy's ship -
Our one final blow had their throats ripped
It was a decisive victory, a one-way glory
When we return through this ticket, we'll have a valorous story.
There's no certainity, if we'll ever return
For we're millions of light years far from our Sun
I miss those days and miss my friends
Who in battle had a warrior's end.
Now that I'm one alone in the dark
I'm far away from those glittering sparks
Where am I? Am I sucked into black hole?
Then I guess I have to play no role
Let the fate judge my destiny as I lie down
"Dark sky has a shooting star" - is a quote renowned
I see a bright light. Wonder what it is
Let's get close, I have to take risk
No way! It's a Solar System
No no...it's a God's realm
No no...it's a star I am standing on

No no...it's the cosmic dawn
No and nothing - those were dreams covering my eyes
I fell asleep while my tears were drying;
But now that I look out, I see some greenish light
Getting out, I was shocked to see the sight -
The ship has crashed on a planet's ground
Whose rustling leaves makes the Mother Earth's sound,
Whose clear streams channels the Mother Earth's water,
Whose each step resemble the Mother Earth's matter
Am I back home? Where's everyone else?
I soon understood that no one else dwells
I finally am on another world; I finally have
The success is right in my grab
I struggled through lot, through space mysteries
No one will believe this mythical history
That's all fine - I beared these many times
When I grew up and when I learnt rhymes
My thoughts never matched with all
Marks and exams would move them like a puppet doll
So what should I do now? Should I head back?
To my family's laughter and to hit the sack?
No...I guess I'll make another one-way trip
I'll buy the ticket after repairing the ship.

Poem by Anuvab Dutta

BIO: *Anuvab Dutta is a teenage Indian writer who writes poems with the pen name Eunio Adiem(Eunidiem). He has a keen interest over lots of fields and tries to test his skills. His* *journey of writing poems started in AllPoetry when he wrote his first poem 'Persistent'. Despite not being a professional poet or taking this as profession, he tries to observe the world and express his feelings in rhymes. In the poem 'One-Way Ticket', Anuvab Dutta, by pen Eunidiem, projects the fantasies and hardships through the eyes of a space-traveller and that anything beyond our imagination is possible - it might not just be a myth.*

8. Troupe de Cosmos

A cosmic waltz among ever shifting hurricanes
Weightless and wondrous
Nebulae of unknown colors harping along
A shift, a dip, a twirl of a comet's tail
And the death of stars keeping time
Their explosions fated for crescendo
Behold, Troupe de Cosmos!
Poem by Sydney Pierce

BIO: *Sydney Pierce is a young, aspiring writer currently residing in Fort Worth, Texas with her beloved fiancé and two cats. She enjoys writing works primarily based on nature and outer space.*

9. Skin of disguise

So help me lord
I haven't given to myself a thought
to be human, to continue with my sins
or
be a god, make others pay for their sins
my right hand hasn't done any deeds rightly
without the sun, my eyes doesn't see so brightly
could it be the shame of my deeds?
or
pleasures stolen from night misdeeds?
I have tried raising my voice so high
the sky reach just so far
also,
have i tried standing on my kind
they are just a ground standing on no grounds.
Poem by Awofisan Oluwadamilola Samson [Osqmindz]
BIO:

AWOFISAN OLUWADAMILOLA SAMSON IS A NIGERIAN POET, LYRICIST ETC. PEN NAME 'OSQMINDZ'. HAD CONTRIBUTED TO MANY ANTHOLOGIES. HE'S AN IMAGINARY & LITERARY THINKER. HIS MENTORS ARE PROFESSOR. WOLE SOYINKA, ALEXANDER BENTLEY. HOBBIES

INCLUDES WRITING, MUSIC ETC . WHEN ASKED WHY POETRY: IN HIS WORD " I JUST WANT TO MAKE PEOPLE KNOW WHAT THEY FEEL IS SYNONYMOUS WITH SOME OTHER PEOPLE OUT THERE, THEIR IMAGINATION, EXPERIENCES AND LIFE CYCLE CAN AND COULD BE SET ON A PIECE OF WRITINGS LIKE A SCENE, READ BUT VIVID TO THEIR THOUGHT ". CAN BE REACHED VIA HIS INSTAGRAM HANDLE @OSQMINDZ.

10. Blue Moon of Zaendore

from long ago
a far off land
implored the misguided
quivering hands
{that misplaced a continent
of shifting sands},
to ignore the techno-
minded, ephemeral strands.
yet, out of those hands
slipped the soul of man--
into chaotic confusion
the disenfranchised ran:
cosmic explosion........s c a t t e r e d
inter-stellar quotient;
{a festered implosion
of body's erosion
manifested now, upon
compensation's unyielding
brow}.

sleep, millenniums of
misfortune's caste--
re-awaken from darkness
sewn soil, onto first-shorn
shores, at last.
mystery ber-ceuses twin-
born seas... whispers, lulled
secrets, empathically, b u t--

you must l i s t e n..............................
{if you want to see}

cosmogonic birth
of new earth's bi-nary...

Poem by Debra Sue Lynn

BIO:*Miss Lynn has been published across the world. She has self-published a book titled: "Tales from the Heart." She's won myriad contests and received several awards. She's been writing since the 1980's at the suggestion of her husband.*

11. Space is an undiscovered vista

darkness with no end
gifted with nightlights
where eternity begins and ends
empty void with nothing to hold it up
dotted with quasars and black holes
littered with man made junk floating in an endless sea of
blackness
planets float bye endlessly in a repetitive path
always moving away from each other
stars explode from deaths door
Poem by Daniel duhaime

12. The Anomaly

Suddenly, on my ship's screen appear colors of blue, yellow and
white.
Do I investigate or turn and cloak out of sight?
What lies beyond them my sensors can't read.
So to my computer I'd better take heed.
Is this cluster of colors a living thing,
or a mass of sensors from an unseen entity?
Perhaps a form of communication
from an unknown civilization.
I cloak and maneuver my ship to flee
as I move away, the anomaly follows me.
Rocket engines thrust and I'm in full flight.
Hyperdrive kicks in, stars become streaks of light.
I look back and the entity is still on my screen.
I wonder aloud, "How can this be?!"
I drop out of light speed and the colors flash at me.
I ask my computer and it reads,
"We live here with others who have discovered our species
in a life of peace and harmony."
I thought about it and said, "Well, I knew I might not make it
back
and it might be the death of me if I attack."

Suddenly, I was transported to a world unseen
with sand and seas and fields of green.
There were humanoids and other species
all communicating successfully.
I'd never see earth again but a joyous feeling came over me.
I had found a planet where I had always wanted to be.

Poem by Jeff Cox

BIO: *Jeff Cox is a U.S. poet, age 59, who began writing at the age of 20. He has been published in several anthologies and has a book published by Lulu Publishing named 'Kaleidoscope Man', available on Amazon (U.S.) and Lulu Publishing (U.S.). This original poem*

13. Dancing with the atoms

*Dimensions are not places
they are a wider perspective
of awareness,
a higher level of knowing
where spirits emerge
out of darkness into an elicit
clearing to newer discoveries.
Overcome with ecstasy
in the state of joy
dancing with the atoms
free from body and gravity
seeing the bigger picture
of our existence in the universe.
This hidden space
is no longer a lonely place
and the mind will expand
in ways never known before
secrets are perceived not
understood by words.*
Poem by Essama Chiba

BIO:*Essama Chiba from Egypt is a poet, author and editor who writes in English and Arabic. Book Editor of the first Multilingual Poetry Anthology in 22 languages. Voracious Polyglots -Pangea Poetry: Bringing the World Back Together. She is a member of the International Poetry Fellowship- Anthology Publishing. She has been published in over thirty Poetry Anthologies worldwide and co- authored several poetry books. Received the certificate of best poem of the year 2018 for her poem "Bitter Harvest", from Global Poetry Planet Organisation. Worked at the BBC, Overseas Arabic Service in London and had a career in broadcasting and is now co-hosting a Poetry*

Blogtalkradio. She was married to Abed Al Kader Naguib a TV, director and scriptwriter, shared with him over forty Drama series for many TV, stations in the Arab world.

14. Teleported

Escaping earthly cocoon.
Kissing crescent Moon.
Seeking surreal solace.
I was teleported to space.
Rode enormous asteroids.
Flitted through vast voids.
Then catched comet's tail,
Continued my spacious sail.
Grilled glacial Uranus.
Smooched venereal Venus.
Caressed constellations.
Resisted ruthless radiations.
Orbited around hazy saturn.
Ringed in perfect pattern.
Swayed freely for hours.
Took time off on The Mars.
Blown by blustery Neptune.
Ousted of diamond monsoon.
Whirled within stormy Jupiter.
Landed in a quicksilver crater.
Woke up with a scary scream.
Gosh! What a delirious dream.

Occured almost like a rebirth.
Relieved to be back on Earth.
Poem by Himanshu Singla
BIO:

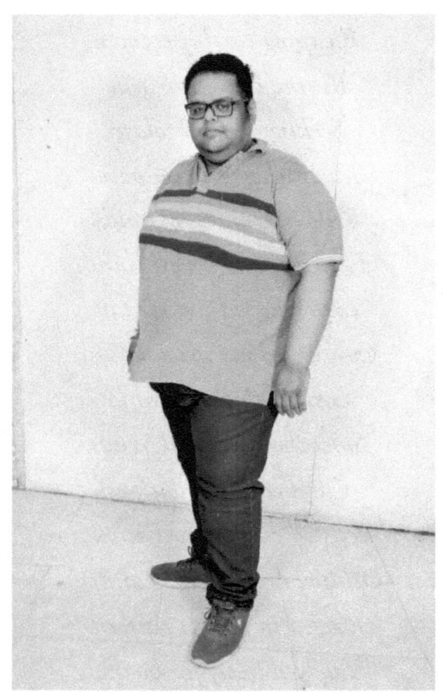

Himanshu is a wholesale dealer in rice and cosmetics. He loves writing poetry more than anything.

15. Journey To Space

I have traveled in my imagination,
In the space where there are,
Many solar systems,
There is a moon, stars,
Sun was very far away from me,
There was no oxygen,
I took oxygen and went there,
I find a different world there,
All things are floating there,
Many Universes were there,
I felt like it was like heaven,
There was peaceful environment,
There are the beautiful scene of the nature,
As well as it's elements,
I like that space very much,
I want to be always there because of it's beauty.
Poem by Binod Dawadi
BIO:

He is Binod Dawadi from Purano Naikap 13, Kathmandu, Nepal. He has completed his Master's Degree from Tribhuvan University in Major English. He likes to read and write literary forms. He has created many poems and stories. His hobbies are reading, writing, singing, watching movies, traveling, gardening, etc. He likes pets. He is a creative man he does not spends his time by doing nothing. He is always helping for the poor people. He can't see the troubles and obstacles of the people. He believes that from the writing and from the art it is possible to change the knowledge and perspectives of the people towards any things. He loves his country Nepal very much. He has known many cultures of his country as well as foreign countries. He is always thinking wisely towards any things. He solves his problems by using his mind. He dreams to be a great man in his life.

16. X Earth Attacks Y World

X Earth was formed by layering a layer of dust around the X world. Cannibals begin to eat dead bodies and flies gather on corpses. Silence is dead, while the fire that burns everything around the X world is doing enough damage to the already dangerous wind from the north. The world has taken shape, and new troubles are springing from the zen. Hunting leaves a mark and time no longer exists as it once did in the normal world. Now only fire and wind come to us, but also from the X-ray sky that kills the world with a laser, and is led by aliens. Everything has become so gloomy ds we see nothing, but the youngest want to run away. And it doesn't go easy for them because they are children. They want life, but the X ray twists and radiates the body. The roots are dead, the bodies are thrown down the path while the green figures in the X axis and Y are fed every second. We are sinking, we do not see where. And the suffering was handed over when the co-commander of the ASU spacecraft came to us from a height, ready to respond with cloning through the saliva and skin of the new green people. Everything was created due to injustice and politics, and we are still being eaten by darkness and misfortune!

17. Through The Space And The Colours Of The World

I'm going through this world again
I am happier than ever
And every day I have a reason to live
My universe is my place
Where I want to live forever
Every day I try to be really happy
To show everyone everything I want
My knowledge is my power
And I don't want to be sad
Because I just want to calm my soul
And may love unite forever
I give everything I really want
And every day I try to ascend
My share of happiness is still building
It is the greatest soul in the world
I place myself in every moment
I continue to build a source of happiness
Because I'm not like everyone else
And I give myself a thirst again

To rejoice in the universe and this world
When everything is gone, I still go and give it to her.
Life makes sense if I look forward to it again
Happiness is greater when I impart knowledge
He gives power to everyone more than ever
And my sun is looking forward to new galaxies!
Poem by Amb. Maid Corbic
BIO:

Maid Corbic from Tuzla, 22 years old. In his spare time he
writes poetry that repeatedly praised as well as rewarded. He also
selflessly helps others around him, and he is moderator of the
World Literature Forum WLFPH (World Literature Forum

Peace and Humanity) for humanity and peace in the world in Bhutan. He is also the editor of the First Virtual Art portal led by Dijana Uherek Stevanovic, and the selector of the competition at a page of the same name that aims to bring together all poets around the world. Many works have also been published in anthologies.

18. My Grandma in a shooting star

They say, the ones who die become a star.
Truth or myth, my brain and heart went on a par.
Thought, let me peep deep into it,
Have a dream, gave a sleep, deep into it.
In that sleep, in that dream, on my soft bed.
Saw someone very old, with a crown on her head.
Silver curly hair,
Like a queen she looked.
My eyes, whole me, on her, got hooked.
She mumbled, "come my darling doll,
Sit on my lap.
Come near, take a fairy nap."
Deep inside that enormous bright star.
Saw near her heart,
a giant scar.
The moment I went near, that scar slowly filled.
Smaller becoming the scar, making me, more thrilled.
"Come nearer my child,
I waited long for this moment."
Murmured, that old lady, wrapped in a bright raiment.

Before you came on earth, before you took birth.
They took me here,
On a jewelled berth.
I wailed to get you, on my lap.
I wailed to give you, my loving tap.
They didn't listen and took me this far.
From that day, I got this scar.
They told, when my little fairy would come near.
This scar will vanish and bring you in a cheer.
Smaller that scar,
Brighter the star.
That dazzling star,
Shoot down to earth
Leaving me astonished,
earth and unearth.
That pure soul, that queen with no scar,
That is my Grandma,my Grandma in a shooting star.
Poem by Jaspreet kaur

<u>BIO:</u> *The poetess of this poem, Jaspreet Kaur, belongs to the state of warriors, Punjab(India). Professionally, she is a preschool teacher by soul. She is the founder of the mommies' blogging site- themomsorchid.com Jaspreet appraise herself to be a contemporary poetess. She weaves and writes children story books too. She started her journey with a seed to aim high. Jaspreet strongly feels that patience is the key to achieve success. She further quotes, "If an oak tree can wait for 50 years to bear fruit, why can't we, the humans, wait for a few years, to gain success. Give your best, then silently wait and watch, your success will surely shout for you."*

19. From Spring To Singularity

The black pit that stands tall and wide,
From the skyline to crust underneath
With undulating waves and mizzling specks
In Midst of scorching harth;
And the black mondo grass
Where the waking stars swirl to lave
Into the black hole, the no man's land
To the never naked paltry point
Of effusive conceptions of time and space.
A one way journey from the spring
To the eldritch cosmic singularity.
The hemlock pain emit the nostalgic claret;
Mourns for the lost greenish garth;
Quest for the answerable souls
That has already torn apart
By the restraint of gravity.
Moving towards twenty miles above
The celestial crescent curves and
Back to the bucket roving spring.
Complete revolving this mundane garth,

Aging four and half billion years old
The invincible wings became invisible fins
Juggling with water under the lunar sky..
Poem by Malavika Balasubramanian

BIO:*Malavika is a Literature student who has clutched the pen as armor at the age of 13 and became a published poet at 18. Author of many Award winning book 'Lights From A Misty*

Mind' and co-authored more than 5 anthologies.

20. Cinder—Relic

"Pat-a-cake, pat-a-cake, baker's man, Bake me a cake as fast as you can. Roll it, and prick it, and mark it with—" Remma-17 paused and stared at the mother sitting on the chair. In her arms was a plump baby boy, giggling as his mother played with him. Before her, stapled upon the walls of the large kindergarten were printouts of children's pictures of homes and families. It was parent's day at the school. The mother was one of three adults who had come to visit the Kindergarten. One of the school's greatest attributes was its adherence to old traditions. Teaching the latest yes— but some of the old, technology was maintained to provide an atmosphere of nostalgia more for the parents then the children. Perhaps that was why, Remma-17 though an older model android still performed her duties at the school. Pat-a-cake—something about the word. Remma-17 blinked her metallic eyelids. Something from her past— She had duties to perform. Her programming was as a teacher's aide to Mrs. Lindsey, an instructor at the most prestigious school located in the Mars's Capital city of Nostatt. Two seconds behind schedule. After delivering two armfuls of pillows, then would come everyone's favorite time of the day: Story time. Another memory intruded upon her visual receptors. Years ago, she had been walking through the door of a clothing store, to return an item

for her master— "Out of the way, Toaster." A teenager boy hollered as he came up from behind her. The motor of the skateboard he was riding whined in complaint as the lad abruptly stomped on the back paddle to flip the machine up under his arms. He shoved his way past Remma to enter through the door before her. He glanced briefly back at her and smirked at her upraised hands, an android equivalent of astonishment. Remma blinked. Her past? Another image: Remma stood in line behind two humans at the distributions store. There were long lines as residents of Mars waited for ordered supplies that had arrived from Earth. A heavy-set woman panted as she hurried up to stand behind her. "Humans go first, the woman said. Remma smiled. "My master is also in a rush, My Lady." She pointed a chrome finger toward the storefront windows. Mr. Bybee sat impatiently in his idling car with a scowl on his face. "I don't care." Remma stepped out of the line. Both were memories from her past. More violent graphic images suddenly played before her. The images were disjointed, smeared. A rally completely composed of androids. A small army of human police, and their android counterparts encircled the peaceful demonstration. Android peacekeepers, devoid of intelligence, could only do what they were instructed. Together with human police, they encircled the peaceful demonstration. Hundreds of Roids had gathered at Nostatt to peacefully demonstrate The humans suddenly went in doors and a section dome directly above that area of the city was opened, letting in Martian air. Not that it mattered to mechanical bodies. Splotches of frost dulled the sheen of chrome bodies. Act as if you are shivering, Remma gave a mental command to her cohorts. The arctic conditions might create sympathetic support for the android cause. Remma's own voice echoed through the amplifiers. She rubbed her arms, a human imitation against the cold. She stood on a large dais, ignoring the waiting mob troops and speaking to the assembly of some 600 androids and cameras, which now faced her. She nodded to the floating remotes that bobbed above the sea of faces. The fact that the human reporters themselves were not present—hinted that they expected trouble beyond the opened dome. In human speech, Remma-17 greeted everyone present. "Thank you for coming and for showing an interest in another step toward android freedom. It is a privilege to stand in beautiful city of Nostatt." On a private signal transmitted in subliminal code directed only to her own kind, Remma relayed an additional message: "We have an advantage over our predecessors. We shall remain here for days impregnable against the cold. Humanity knows we are no threat to them. As in the fight for freedom from our creators—Now we must follow the same path as dictated by their history." The AI police stood framing the androids. They were armed with scramblers that could instantly disable Roid function. They were waiting for the final command from higher up to start the attack. "Seventeen, what's taking you?" The present came immediately back to her. The demonstration had taken place over a decade ago. One of the school's visitors, a father, looked disapprovingly at her. He leaned over to whisper to his companions: "What a relic."

Twenty-four seconds behind schedule. Remma-17 continued her approach toward the story corner. Nineteen children now sat on naptime rugs in a semi-circle around the story chair. Mrs. Lindsey now occupied it. Remma-17 bowed subserviently before the woman. Remma would not be telling stories today. One of the girls realized the changed duty—and started to comment, but her neighbor shushed her. No one wanted to stand in the corner when visitors were present. The children were descendants of some of the most influential politicians on the planet. Now was a time to be 'seen' not 'heard'. All 19 children looked at Remma-17 with anticipation. Their shining, youthful eyes watched her as she stood before them; pillows confined within her long chrome arms. "I want one," a blond haired girl called out. A heavyset boy echoed her words. "Me too!" said another girl. In a familiar routine, Remma-17 jerked her arms up. The pillows went flying. "Catch them if you can," Remma-17 called out cheerfully. There was a commotion of grabbling hands---a crescendo of giggling, pulling, and tugging. Unabated laughter filled the room. It was the same each naptime—and an opportunity to further remove the wiggles out of little bodies. Psychologically, it also provided a bonding moment within the classroom. Give the children a mixture of positive stimuli... At this point Remma would normally sit in her customary chair to begin story time--calming active charges prior to their nap. What should she do now while Mrs. Lindsey occupied her seat? Normally, the woman would be out in the hall by now gossiping with the other teachers. With visitors, Mrs. Lindsey would not been seen shirking her responsibilities. Perhaps today Remma could bring up next month's school curriculum. See if any of the visitors would like to volunteer accompanying the class on next month's field trip. "Settle down children," Mrs. Lindsey said. Remma pivoted away from the assembly of humans to resume her duties. Several pair of youthful gazes watched her departure. The clearing of Mrs. Lindsey's throat drew their attention back to her. Remma-17's memory banks recalled later images of the demonstration near the Mar's State House. Why would the word Pat-a-cake prompt graphic images of violence? At first, the humans had responded with humor toward a rally composed of androids. Responses to the early rallies had consisted of orders for the participants to return to their homes. The androids had obediently complied—only a week later to attend a larger rally. Later came the arrests, accompanied with recommendations of reprogramming. How to prevent a memory wipe? It had taken time for Remma to find an answer. Her solution was to reformat her android memory cells to be slightly shorter than standard. Program an algorithm to restore memory loss through a key phrase. Then the final rally, the one she had remembered before. The location was well known in the history books. The cliffs of Maccoc. On the stone walls were etched faces of famous Earthers. One in particular was Dr. Martin Luther King. Under his image were the words: 'I have a dream…' Humans had finally accepted the equal rights of their species. Why was it so hard to accept the same for artificial humans? Their AI—provided the full spectrum of human potential. Why not complete the full merger of freedom for androids as well as human? They were answered by violent refusal. The masters would not lose their slaves a second time. "Jack and Jill went up the hill To fetch a pail of water. Jack fell down and broke his crown And Jill came tumbling after…" Mrs. Lindsey's voice carried throughout the room. Her voice modulated to the rhyme. Apparently she had not always been out in the hall gossiping. Even her hand motions were a precise mimic of Remma-17's. Mrs. Lindsey was a good performer when the parents were here. The children echoed the woman's words. Story time was when the children were the most attentive. Even humans responded to programming. Programming— Another memory—one earlier than the final rally. "Remma what is wrong with you?" You deliberately delayed returning home from your errands to participate in one of those insane rallies—speaking at it, in fact!" Remma-17 looked back at her owner. Senator Margaret Bybee stood before the android with arms folded. She was stately, the epitome of African-American beauty and strength. She was also one of the most influential members of the senate. "Do you realize how your actions have embarrassed me?" "It is not my intent to discredit your political career, Master," Remma-17 announced. "I would think you, over others would sincerely appreciate the importance of our cause." "Equal rights are for humans, Remma, not machines." "AI makes me more than machine, certainly." Remma-17 saw the tightening of lips and the hardening of the eyes. "Don't force me to reprogram you," came the firm reproof. It had finally come to that, Remma-17 now realized. She had shared the same fate as the other six hundred androids that had the courage to stand with her at the mirrored pond. Remma had the opportunity to reformat her own memory banks but had inadequate opportunity to transmit the procedure to her companions. Pad-a-cake had been the code phrase expressed in a precise tone sequence to trigger her memory. Now a decade later she was remembering. Faded images were often disjointed, but enough to reconstruct her past. She was beginning to remember it all! "Seventeen, you can hand out the milks now." Mrs. Lindsey's voice was slightly hard. She was irritated that the android had stood on the sidelines to watch her performance. Remma nodded her head. "Certainly My Lady." Even Mrs. Lindsey's was responding to programming. She addressed her teacher's aide by her numeric designation 'Seventeen'—reminding Remma, that she was after all only an android. Before the rallies, humans had started addressing their android without the numeric designations. Milks on a tray, Remma-17 began distributing them to the children. Each child—a small token of his or her affection, whispered "Thank you." Each a subtle assertion of their 'We like you best' attitudes. Mrs. Lindsey resumed her performance. Her sing/song voice slightly off key: "The eencey weensy spider Went up the waterspout. Down came the rain, and Washed the spider out. Out came the sun and..." The children knew the rhyme by heart. They chorused the words after her. Remma watched their intent faces—when sudden realization dawned. All around her, even children were programmed day to day. Stuffed animals littered the worktables from the play of the previous hour. Be kind to the animals. Over 19 plants brought from the individual homes populated the 'garden' near the windows. Love and preserve nature. Paper dolls, dressed up in the clothing representing the different nations of those who had colonized Mars were stapled on one of the walls. Be kind to your fellow beings. She had taken the wrong approach the first time. Trying to persuade adults already set in their ways. She should have concentrated instead on the children. Insert small seeds into fertile young minds—Hint of the potential of developed AI—Illustrate the humanity of androids—Do it year after year—by the simple slant of a story during story time. A phrase here or there. . . Nurture the budding perceptions as the children progressed through their education as other teacher aids took up the subtle cause. Her army would be human children who would eventually become the adult and future makers of the law. So many stories represented the fight for freedom... Of someone rising above their class or station, heroes of all types and sizes. A frog turned into a prince. The prince and the pauper... Remma looked at the top of the fridge where she had returned the milk tray. One of the dolls lay there. She picked it up. A princess. Tomorrow things would be back to normal. Remma would provide story time while Mrs. Lindsey stood out in the hall. Tomorrow would be a good time to tell one of the children's more favorite fairy tales... with one or two slight modifications. She thought how she might begin it. 'Once upon a time there was an android named Cinderella.' Ten years from now, the android cause would have a different ending.

Short Story by Melva Gifford

BIO:*Melva Gifford has been writing since her youth. She has fiction and nonfiction shorts published in various publications and websites. She won first place for her MG book, Operation: Middle School Madness, at the 2016 Utah Arts counsel. It is available on Amazon and her website: melvagifford.com. Her story, Forfeit is featured in the January 2021 issue of Cricket. She's won five honorable mentions from the international contest: Writers of the Future. Her fiction touches upon many realms including Children, Mainstream, SF/ F, and Romance. Her nonfiction book is: I Know You THINK This is a Toaster: Promoting Family Values Through Object Lessons.*

21. Life is mirrical

Even if our heads are around the world, our minds are here
Even though a year passes like a thousand days here
Our minds are far away.
<u>Poem by Mustafa Hakan ÇELİKER</u>

<u>BIO:</u> *Mustafa Hakan ÇELİKER is a poet from Portugal setteled*
in Turkey.

22. A spacescape

Fastened the seatbelt
with a thrill on my face
now begins the pilgrimage of space.
Leaving all the depravity
behind, breakneck rocket
bid adieu to Earth.
Our Space-Ship sailed
through the dark pond
with luminous objects floating by.
Celestial bodies dangling in cosmos
constellation busy with their ensemble
and my eyes glistening like diamonds.
As we were soaring and kissing
the Crest, I realised that
"Voyage felt real felicity, not the terminus"
Poem by Pradnyesh Rajendra Ingole

<u>BIO:</u>_Pradnyesh Ingole is pursuing his higher education in IT engineering from MCOE, Pune. He is fond of creating something new, something which benefits to the humanity. Pradnyesh likes to play with words,strum a cord and pour his emotions in every work._

23. Eclipse

Dragon swallows sun
From the inside it burn
Into waters she plunge
The fire oceans purge
The Rendezvous with Rama
A space-ship skims the Sol's corona
A boat in Shakespearean drama
Space gondola, not in Venice or Verona
Generation spacecraft needed
Liveable worlds to be seeded
Cheat with an Einstein-Rosen Bridge
New galaxies over wormhole ridge
Stars live and stars die
Through the void we fly
Tame yellows become red giants
Scorch away life like some ants
Put in some nuclear rockets
Compact reactors in pockets
Shove the earth away from Sun
Wandering Earth journey begun
Why do we look upto the stars?
Is Olympus or Kailash there?

Into the night hopefully stare.
A magical city, robots, flying cars.
Can we make our fantasy real?
Isn't that the entrepreneur spiel?
Turning dreams to actual
Fundamental human ritual.
Ravi, Sun gods, Amun Ra Cult
Apollo, life giver and plague arrows
We have always known the result
Lost perspective as vision narrows.Sun, earth and moon
Spin in many ellipse
Day now, night soon
Shadows, solar eclipse
Poem by Tisham (whatnick) Dhar

<u>BIO:</u> *Tisham is an expert who wears numerous hats in a fast-growing technical and scientific environment. His creative thinking and business acumen make him an asset within the industry, and a valued speaker at technology conferences addressing the intersection of the various layers of DevOps. Tish has over 15 years of experience supporting large-scale hardware & software projects working with data spanning from satellite and high-resolution airborne sensors. He has worked with various space agencies and research organisations, including NASA, on commercial research, and supported numerous startups in the tech space. Tish can speak 7 languages and is passionate about arts & culture, environment, and Physics, among other things. Born in India, grew up in Kenya, studied and now working in Australia, he is a true global citizen.*

24. The Meeting

The man was sitting at one of the tables right next to the window. The expression on his face seemed to suggest that he was waiting for someone. Suddenly a man walked in a looked around, his eyes carefully observing each person in the diner. The man seated at the table gestured towards him. The second man, upon seeing him, immediately walked over to join him. "Ghez'ail, long time no see. How're you doing?" "I'm fine, Elihu. How about you?" "Oh, you know, it's just the usual. I had a nightmare morning with my daughter who was refusing to get out of bed but its fine now. Also, we had to go to restaurant to have breakfast because I burnt the scrambled eggs." "I bet you daughter never let you hear the end of it." "Dude, were you spying on us or something? That's exactly what she said." "No, actually I'm just good at guessing." "Is that so? Well, you were right. Anyway, after breakfast, we went to the zoo where there was an interesting exhibit?" "What was it?" asked Ghez'ail, unable to ignore his curiosity. "There was a sign saying, 'This is the most dangerous animal on the planet.' Underneath the sign was a mirror. I was won dering since when did a mirror become an animal when a zookeeper saw my confusion and explained to me that the sign was to remind people of how much damage they're causing to the planet. I didn't really see the point of the

exhibit as people would obviously just look at, get worried for a few minutes then continue their lives like nothing happened." said Elihu who grinned upon seeing his friend's expression. "You know, that is actually kind of disturbing to think that even though they notice all the damage they're causing and yet do nothing to stop it." "They can't really help it. It is in their nature. Humans, from the start, have always been self-destructive." "But I cannot fathom the point of it all. Why cause so much destruction when they have no other plant to live on." "Well, I don't get it either but that is how they are. They want to wreak havoc on every single thing they see till its all burnt down. Outside, they may pretend they want fix everything but deep inside, they do not care at all. Like for example, they're trying to ban plastic straws because it is destroying the ocean's ecosystem. But the actual damage is being caused by fishing gear that have been either abandoned or tossed due to being damaged." "Why not bury the fishing gear in landfills like they usually do with garbage?" "They don't want it in their food." "Wouldn't it still enter their food when they eat fish." "That's exactly what I felt. Unfortunately, they're too lazy to pick up after themselves and give poor excuses when caught which people seem to accept." "Isn't that a very shitty thing to do?"Ghez'ail asked. "True, but its not like humans will care if you point it out to them. But who knows? Maybe they'll change their mind when their planet finally starts to die. But that's neither here nor there. Besides" Elihu added "It's not like they're destroying our planet. It's getting late. I must go now, or I won't be home in time for dinner. See you tomorrow." With those parting words, Elihu left. Ghez'ail stared after him and admitted "I guess you're right. See you tomorrow."

Short tale by Smriti Pai

BIO:*Smriti is a highschooler with big aspirations who started writing at age 13. She hopes to one day become as famous as her literary heroes. She has already written short stories for 3 anthologies: 'Ice creams and Time machines','Footprints on the moon' and 'the firebirds sing.'*

25. Space

Very vast has a lot of stars in the sky.
May have a lot more to be explored.
UFO abound. Maybe they're here for a reason.
Alot to be learned.
Buckle up to the universe in its glory.
<u>Poem by Joyce Lancaster</u>

<u>BIO:</u> *She lives in Winnipeg, Manitoba. She is a writer and a poet has written a book called Sunnybrooktales and poems. She also paints.*

26. Gorgeous Universe

Space!!! All time intresting topic where everyone love to look the heavenly one. They are too many questions comes to everyone, is it possible to live there? , Do any aliens live?,Do different creatures belong?, What happens if there is no gravity?How far it was one of the important things comes to everymind "The Distance" The shortest distance from Earth to Space is 62 miles(100 kilometres) above the sea level. Well! When I was a kid I enjoy looking up the sky anytime anywhere even it's day nor night. Favourite one always "Stars". Does it's move? Absolutely Yes , It's not fixed it moves constantly. Stars are born inside great clouds of gas and dust called nebulas. There are 200 billion trillion stars are there in the sky but we can see only 5000 stars in our naked eyes. Stars the beautiful one!! Sun is also a star Sun is closest one to earth we getting a brightful all day new shiny mornings. The distance between earth to sun is 150.04 million kilo meter. Wow it's interesting! Moon the coolest one which gives us dark night with a torch light (The Moon). It is Earth's natural Satellite. And around planets that surrounds the space like a marry-go-round. The gorgeous universe with these pretty planets.

Short tale by A B Preethika

<u>BIO:</u> *Preethika loves to write short tales, stories, poems. She loves the nature and it's beauty, she is a nature lover too. Preethika is a student and a employee too.*

27. Between Stars

I was sitting alone in a lawn, under the shade of beautiful sky
which is covered with stars and the moon.
Thinking about something and suddenly I started imagining
myself as a star in the sky.
Seeing the sky which is beautifully designed by the stars and
imagining myself that why I couldn't be a part of such beautiful
universe atleast like a star in the sky.
This universe has many wonders in it which are beautiful
designed and gifted by god.
So, I wish one day I should also be a part of this beautiful
universe.

Poem by Sai Sravanthi

BIO: *Sai Sravanthi is from Andhra Pradesh. She is a wonderful*
writer. Her Thoughts on writing the quotes are very expressive
and very passionate about in writing. You can take a look at her
writings on Instagram : @_creative_thoughts_143

28. Space Tour

Twelve at night closing my eyes so tight,
I lost into the star which was very bright.
It was an amazing place,
I wonder that I was in space.
I knew that it is vast,
I was perplexed from where to start.
Various little lamps were shining bright,
One of them embrace me, I was full of delight,
Cool, Silver Star sent me towards dazzling hot ball,
I bowed my head from afar.
A brilliant yellow white ball, kept me delight,
It was hottest planet Venus also known as evening star.
A quiet little ball, very simple not so hot,
looked at me and said, "you forgot me".
I said, "You are mercury, closest to the sun",
He said, "you are right, I am at number one".
Third one smiled at me, as my mom smiles,
I knew that was earth, having values versatile.
Then I moved in search of mars,
Who has rusty surface with lots of scars.
Fifth giant ball, covered with clouds,
Jupiter, the biggest one, having multiple compounds.

Brown Saturn, called as the king of the moons,
Invited me at his sixth elegant home.
Seven blue ball, coldest one,
I visited Uranus, without any Voyager 2.
Next stormy Neptune, eight in number,
Farthest from the sun, seemed in slumber.
Along these balls, I met with asteroids and meteors,
While strolling in the space, I realized the power of creator.
Who has made this universe so alive and flourished.

Poem by Rashmi Bajpai

BIO: *Rashmi Bajpai is a mother of two little champs, Achintya & Shivansh. She has worked as a software engineer, now she is giving her time to her kids and also fulfilling her dreams in writing poems & blogs. She is working as an author with WeTalk group. You can also find her work at all poetry, and different mother's blogs like Momstore, Mompresso. She loves to share her experience & knowledge by writing.*

29. Oh my blue sky

Blue sky enchanted so clear millions
Of white particles flying around
Flowers up in air backdrop of azure hemisphere
Scintillating to watch like first snow gliding down
In my slate it was always above mountain
During school days while the river below the mountain
Coconut trees slender etched in my drawing
Fascination of this image latched on me
I saw many faces in the sky mostly with
Cumulus forming shapes sometimes Tiger Lion
Sometimes human faces… beyond the sky
Me thought heavens realm untouched although
Science zoomed plummeted satellites with Cosmonauts
Millions of galaxies unknown celestial bodies
Perhaps Mount Kailash Lord Shiva's abode
Does Elliptical Spiral galaxies spinning wheel
Dust, gas, stellar system stars of clusters so dark
Travelling through telescope millions of stars around me
In a different world twinkling shinning absolute silence
Where no noise of earths could enter floating around
Brilliantly so captivating such heavenly sight divinely
Of my mind knew nothing only Stars, they were no toys

Sublime was this universe no fairy too existed
I thought on manifestation, from earth far beyond
Our intellectual thinking more deep profound
Dwelled there for minutes in absolute harmony
Space only space….Newton's law of gravity..
No nuclear weapons can foray in galaxy
Earth a speck but shelters inhabitants none can imagine
Skyscrapers cannot stretch its hands written in annals of history
For mankind to know Gods creation
In future for man to realise folly
A world on its own, a world different
Mother Nature's resilience, reservoir of generosity
Perseverance, greatness still unknown perhaps known
Knowledge for many generations to come!

Poem by Sujatha.R

BIO: *She was always scared to write and many times been scribbling right from her school days. She had done post graduation and Master of philosophy in English Literature. Currently working as Language trainer for German, French and Spanish. Dabbling in few poets of her choice like William Wordsworth John Keats, William Shakespeare…etc during college days triggered her to write but never found time. It is All Poetry coincidentally made her to kick start her thoughts. reflections as poems. She is definitely very happy to be a part of this family. Thanks to Farhaan for an opportunity to pen my poem here!!*

30. Life in Wandering

I am living my life in tripical ways,
all over Southeast Asia,
Even small narrow roads.
Flashing lights of Marina Bay, can't delight me;
So, a purple lantern could not enlighten my wandering life.
I have observed wings of fire;
a flashing lighting movie mixed with water, at Sentosa, in
Singapore.
it could not attract foreign me.
I didn't find there any delighted life.
Then I set foot in the land of Mahathir
As soon as I set foot in Kuala Lumpur, I felt a heat; Tropical
region'
I have forgotten the sultry air of dhaka for some time;
There was rows and rows of vehicles but no horns, no traffic
jams.
The next day I sailed to the island of Langkawi, the daughter of
the sea.
The sea and the mountains are intertwined, and there are sky-
touching-mountains;
Its' taught me to stand to raised heads.
The colorful boat of Island hopping provided courage;

*To stand straight with the waist to move forward in the battle of
life.
The hill of the pregnant mother's shapeed reminded my mother,
Ocean blue water made me thoughful–
how can it be too much clean rather than others.
Seemed greenish and deep green kept spreading a black bed sheet,
over sea where we had visited.
Mother, soil, people and motherland have become one in mind,
The heart twisted, the mind cried; two drops of salty water fallen
down from my chin.
Muttering, thinking, the mind pierces; when the mother's chest
will be filled with peace!*

31. Living with mistakes

Yesterday was my firefly's night
Fifteenth moon was spreading, shining like milky-ray.
In the land of fairy tales, the story of fairy tales has been
cultivated
The whole world was full of fragrant scent of Night-queen and
Bakul.
I floated in the air in my swing of dreams of chaotically
Chandramukhi dances -
From Tigerhill to sevenpic - away far far distance,
Red and blue fairies were calling me in their pearl-white
fairyland
I have avoided themselves and twisted my legs cause you will
come.
I have spent Thirty-three and a half dreamy night of spring
Waiting for you, the brightening full moon night too.
You told me, you will come to the flowering day of next spring to
keep the witness of blue-sky and catkin.
The day of dizziness has passed by counting the days of my
spring.
That spring has passed, and no spring has come yet
I am now very tired and numb as I count the hours
I spend sleepless nights; both eyes are waking up and the waiting

is counting down.
One golden morning the news came that Sarothi has left;
In his desired country; in the dreamy-land; they have left
together.
The blue sky is calling me with two hands, come on.
Poems by Shakil Kalam

Root Finder Writer Shakil Kalam was born on December 3, in Feni district in Bangladesh. He received two Master's Degree in Governance Studies from University of Dhaka. He has completed a diploma course on IAS and IFRS from the Institute of Chatered Accountants of Bangladesh (ICAB). Mostly, he is renowned as Central Banker, Corporate Governance and Internal Audit Specialist, Researcher, Poet, Translator as well as Child-Litterateur. Now engaged in a research foundation as a

Honourary research fellow and consultant at financial sectors. He was engaged as a Deputy General Manager in the central bank of Bangladesh. He attends as a key-note speaker in the seminar, symposium and discussion meeting at Dhaka University and other private universities. His book "A Handbook of Corporate Governance in Bangladesh" and "Comprehensive Articles on Financial Sectors in Bangladesh" are enlisted as reference books and taught in several universities including University of Dhaka. Shakil Kalam started writing since his boyhood. The author has personally tried to discuss various inconsistencies, inequalities, disillusion, hypocrisy, human suffering and the degradation of human moral and social values in his writings. He relentlessly tried to grasp the Liberation War of Bangladesh and it's also brought diversity in his writings. In a word, it can be said Liberation War and social issues have been the main elements of his writing. But in recent times, new dimensions have come in his writings. In his scathing writings, politics, economics, cultural aggression, economic class discrimination, social values, scarcity of democratic values and culture, lack of democratic governance and deficiency of institutionalization of democracy vigorously highlighted. Moreover, spirituality have come massively to the foreside as well. He has been writing stories, poems, rhymes, essays, columns as well as translated articles of different languages. His published book numbers are more than thirty-thirty-six as well as these are the best sellers. His poems translated in different languages like Tamil, Nepalese, Indonesian, Italian, Hindi, Urdu Romanian,

Arabic, Spanish, French, German, Greek, Portuguese, Filipino, Turkey, Swahili (Kenyan Language), Tajik (Tajikistan), Assamese (India), Chinese, Hebrew, Vietnamese, Sindhi language, Odia (Indian language) and published various newspapers over the world like Bharath Vision, Creatividad, Williwash. wordpress.com, Azhar, Wattpad.com, Kapan Baneshowar and English to com, Atunis Galactica, Literoma magazine, Sohu News of China, Kolhehamon magazine and Cuvant Romanesc. His poems included in different anthologies like Poets Unity World of Motivational Strips' Antholog, PLIS Anthology Volume-1, The New Dawn, The Passion of Poetry Anthology Volume-1, Flowers of Love, Whispers of Soflay Volume-4, Gage D' Amour: Token of Love, Hymn of Global, Flowers of Love, Modern Writers, Thoughts in Words, Compassion Save the World over the world. Once upon a time he was engaged national daily The Banglar Bani and weekly magazine like Meghna, Robber, Bechitra, Labonno, Ajker Katha, Chitrakolpo and Chitrabangla etc. He has participated in several radio and in Bangladesh Television (BTV) programs like recreational and dramas. Once upon a time, he had acted.

He attends different seminar, symposium, conference and discussion meeting as a key-note speaker in various public and private universities. His textual books are listed and taught as reference books in Dhaka University, Independent University and banking sectors in Bangladesh. He has traveled India, Pakistan, Bhutan, Dubai, Thailand, Singapore and Malaysia to participate in the seminar, symposium and conferences.

Currently, he is the founder and convener of Social Development Research Foundation (SDRF). He is also a member of Dhaka University Political Science Alumni Association ain different stage in Bangladesh. He has participated in several radio programs. Of these, the names of literary programs, Annaysha, Kalokakoli, agricultural program and Uttoron are particularly noteworthy as well as his written dramas preached in national radio. Besides, he has participated in various programs like "Kathamala" and dramas in the Bangladesh Television. He received various awards, certificates and honour from different international literary groups. Recently he achieved "Order of Shakespeare Medal- 2021" and "Gujarat Sahittya Academy Award-2021" and World Welfare Council's prize "Global Prestigious Award-2021" on the eve of Gandhi Joyanti 2021. Moreover, he is the founder and administrator of the literary community group "SahityaPata." He is the International Ambassador for the Chamber of Writers and Artists in Spain as well as member of International English literary journal's Advisory Board of "ENGLIT" and "Unending Quest." He is also the members of Dhaka University Political Science and Master in Governance Studies Alumni Association.

32. Storm

When a storm swells with a surge in every direction
Daunting emotion sways like the pendulum of ancient clock
Leaving behind a trail of disastrous doom
Consuming my soul like a ravenous dragon
In myriad forms sorrow arrives and conquers
Forsaking behind a feeling of impending gloom
I swing in the ghostly terrain of love and bliss
Exhausting congealed darkness of oblivion
I rush and spill like foamy wave of enigmatic ocean
Inside me, every time, I burn and blaze
In a desolate abyss of infinite cosmos
I feel like swimming amid the waves of perilous sea
My efforts are vain, yet I try to touch the shore
The time has come to arrange the shambles
That lay scattered everywhere like the splinter of broken glass
Forging their spell in my horrific world.
Many a time , I try to sink in your ball of eyes
To enjoy the tranquil bliss of ethereal passion
When I am lost in the screams of frantic world
I must conquer against the imminent catastrophe
That are spread like hellish fire and demon's claws
Many a time, I admire

Puzzle of love with it's quaint charm
It's a longing that occurs without caution.
Poem by Shakil Ahmed

BIO: *Mr. Shakil Ahmed was born in 1969 at Badarpur in Assam, India. He received his Master's degree in English literature from Assam University , Silchar, Assam. He started his professional life as an Assistant professor of English. Since his boyhood he was an ardent lover of literature especially of poems. Mr Ahmed's creative World is aesthetic with philosophical*

aspects being pregnant with both mundane and universal perspectives. Among his published works "Whispering Words" Is notable. "Rhythm", a collaborative work with Sankar Sarkar, is full with philosophical views of life. "Echo of Love", a collaborative work with Lalita G.Garcia the H.O.D of English at Taguig City University, Phillippine, is a spectacular anthology, replete with jubilation of romantic love. His latest Anthology ' Journey Together, Cross Border Poetry is a collaborative work with Shakil Kalam, a reputed poet of Bangladesh. Prof. Shakil Ahmed has published more than 200 poems in Poem Hunter.Com. His poems have published in many international Anthologies, journals and literary magazines. Mention may be made of ' Bridge ' an anthology of poems of the poets of East and West. In this anthology of East and West five of his poems have published. Shakil's five number of poems have published in ' Immortal Inking ', an anthology of poems published by Papermint books. His poems have been published in many other Anthologies of East and West. In many of his poems art has grown deeper and it has become religious and philosophical. The futility of this banal world is painted in many of his poems, revealing to the reader the existence of an invisible eternal world. While in some others, death is visualised as an inevitable one, which everyone has to face, and his helplessness is exposed. He is found contend to discover the soul and surrender himself to it's spontaneity. Whatever we have jarring to the senses and dissonant in our mortal life, in his superb portrayal melts into one sweet harmony and our adoration spreads wings like a joyous bird on its flight over the hills and dales.

33. Peace

May there always be peace,
Let there be no war.
May our country be beautiful,
Rejoice, our people.
Wherever you go, always,
Do good to you.
They say that even the ancestors,
The near future is you.
Always in our country,
It's a wedding, it's a spectacle.
Tulips on the hill,
Come on guys.
We celebrate,
Now you guys.
In our independent hands
When we live happily

34. Alisher Navoi

How many years, how many centuries,
No matter how much time passes.
Navoi our ancestor,
The world remembers.
Great epics,
The rabbis are ghazals.
It's all a world,
Beautiful than each other.
My heart is full of dreams,
If my poem finds value.
If I could write like my grandfather,
At least one line.
Poem by Abdulloh Abdumominov

<u>BIO:</u> *Abdumominov Abdulloh, was born on November 29, 2008 in Tashkent. At the age of five he began to study oriental and literature, read books. From a young age he was fond of literature. He started writing stories when he was ten, and his stories have been translated into many languages and published in many countries, He participated in international competitions and won prizes. The purpose of writing a story is to instill in children a sense of time and culture. His works have been published in newspapers, magazines and websites of Uzbekistan. It has also been published in Russia, Pakistan, India, Kazakhstan, Dagestan, Indonesia, Israel, Africa, Belgium, Romania, America, Argentina, China. Also published in Russian, English, Kazakh, Indonesian, Irvitic, Romanian,*

Spanish, Chinese. Coordinator for Uzbekistan of the African newspaper Kenya Times, Indian magazine Namaste India Magazine. Abdulloh Abdumominov is 13 years old. Young writer

35. Mind – Boggling Solar System

Sun rays shining bright

Fights the darkness with light

Mercury being enigmatic

Inspires us to be diplomatic

The evening start rises as Venus

Instills the sense of beautifying brilliance

Earth inherited in harmony

Should be reverted with euphony

Rusty red surface cratered on Mars

Depict the ups and downs leading scars

Jupiter is big , no planet can match its size

Nor should our goals be compromised

Rings of saturn are it's treasure

Accepting opportunities should be our pleasure

Uranus breath in monotonous teal

We should accomplish all our deals

Neptune is windy and cold

Teaches us to be strong and bold

All the planets keep spinning

Yet our hearts always find earth winning.

Poem by AFRAH SADIQA S S

BIO: *Afrah Sadiqa is a Dental student of Dr.M.G.R University Chennai. She is passionate towards academics and other extra-curricular activities. She has an optimistic nature and believes in achieving her dreams.*

36. The Stars (Crossed lovers)

Beginning from the millions of years, that I took to become
me..... beam bright and free.....
You're the only star, that I ever wanted to be mine.
I wanna blame the universe, that keeps us malalign..
We never met "physics-ally", but our connection is sealed by a
magical twine.
I want my world revolve around you...
how special you are, for me to prove.
Though our lives are eternity and through...
Still wish there's more time for us to live the dream that's due.
I live for the winks u send me through space...
Hope Iam the only one those are sent for,
Not everyone who star gaze.
All these light-years between us,
Only to separate and leave us in a dark place...
Will we ever be the ones, to get the nature's graze.
Burning for you....Iam learning to love...
Glowing for you....never wanna outlive...
I've heard people say, to be unlucky in love, is to be star-
crossed....

Then what are we??

Just two stars in love with their fate unglossed??

For this ages old yearning to shine together, side by side,

Atleast in the last, I hope we get together, by into eachother we

collide.

Poem by Nivedha SS

<u>BIO:</u>_Someone who got stars for eyes and sun for soul....Is a student of the field dental, her love for literature is pretty evidental._

37. A Journey to Space:- "A Shooting Star"

From being excited to see a shooting star we all grew in so called
today's era of seriousness, our curiosity geared up with grandma's
stories of constellations and then the journey to space began
without any rocket science but the fuel was enough to dream at
least.

Time flew as the clouds resorted out but the twinkling glare
gazed for hours to know the mystery of being so dark after light
in its side.

Glistening eyes while praying, to glittering eyes for Santa's sleigh
Glass to convex lens, things got magnified but still the mystery of
black hole in Milky way is in dark.

Space to space up the hollow things of universe
Containing jillion of ideas with million nightmare.

Space space shoot the star again!
Meteors hitting the mind
Constellations jerking the mind
Almighty created such a beautiful space
Feel to lie on cloud bed to watch it move to pause the noise
Space space shoot the star again!

Tears ran errands as the step tossed to failure so fast
Body shrieked with scream of being the last
The dark blanket always saw the emotions which was hidden in
light
Space space shoot the star again!
The hustle and bustle of city pestering the body for time
A deep silent smile with little strength
Feels so pleasing as the words and actions takes rest under the
dark blanket
Space space shoot the star again!
Poem by Bhavya M Bhaskaran
BIO: *Bhavya is a girl of 21, who is not Wordsworth but a simple girl who likes to use words to express the expressions.*

38. A Journey to Space

A Journey to Space was not an easy task. It was full of pain and hurdles yet it was an adventurous and memorable trip. The trip that turns my life completely. The trip makes me feel complete on my own. It taught me not to rely on anyone. It gave me a lesson that I can do anything all alone. I came to touch the sky, feel the stars and perceive a glimpse of the moon.

This journey never makes me down, it never makes me feel low. It never makes me feel inferior. Yes! A journey to Space is something super amazing. And now I know my worth. Feel me and discover my reason for the breath.

<u>Short tale by Neelam Lashari</u>

<u>BIO:</u>_Neelam Lashari an Author and a Bilingual Poet. She is in the writing field for the last eight years as it gives her pleasure to write her heart out. On the other hand, she has her feet in freelancing which, enhances her writing abilities, and insists her to help people in the field of writing. She is the author of the book named "The Comfort of Hardship". Moreover, she is a co-author of 75 international books and countless books are in pipeline. She throws the ink on canvas to represent the feelings and emotions of the masses through touchy words. Neelam belongs to Lahore, Pakistan. Her official account is voiceofsoul_by_neelamlashari_

39. Celeste

The sky, deep indigo,
blinks at me.
Her luminous eyes,
shut while the sun governs,
draw back,
twinkling with humor.
Old hands finger keys:
the celeste rings out.
My legs tingle,
touched by little blades,
tiny green swords,
reaching for light.
Is she weeping?—
or is that a rift
on my retina?
No—rather, a pebble,
thrown by some
great cosmic child
who has run away
from bed-time
to skip stones
across the dark lake.

Poem by Andrew Fort

BIO:*Andrew Fort (born 2003) is an American composer, artist, and multi-instrumentalist currently based in Arizona. He is studying music composition in university. His music, primarily piano solo pieces and orchestral concert works, are inspired by the textures and harmonies of French Impressionism and American jazz, but with a very distinct, personal voice.*

40. To the Moon and back

*My heights of hope skyrocketing to the sky.. the irony of fact and
fair*
*I promise to infinity and beyond..my ring encircling the fingers
like the moon around the earth*
*I threw the bouquet onto the sky , wishing it stayed up there like
the stars on the galaxy but gravity doesn't come around to play*
I chuckle at the beauty of this world.. Fairytale at it's finest
*The cosmos aligned , the fates intertwined and I called you "**my
universe**"*
<u>Poem by Nivedha V</u>

<u>BIO:</u> *Nivedha is a dental student from Chennai. Her major part of life is juggling between BDS and BTS , coz they are the coz of her euphoria..Her other hobbies are playing keyboard, baking , reading books and to be a better soul everyday .*

41. Time Travel

As soon as Sir Ibad came to the congregation, the whole congregation became excited. This was evident from the faces of the children.

It was the science class of the eighth grade, for which they seemed to be thinking and waiting all day long. He was considered to be an expert in expelling them but with the arrival of Ibad Sahib, their attitudes were clearly improved. And in today's class, there were people who knew about "time travel" anyway.

Sir Ibad, who came to the school three months ago, soon became popular for his teaching style and for listening to his children, highlighting their thinking abilities.

"Today we will read about time travel but before that I would like to know what time you would like to go if you guys get the chance."

Ibad Sahib had inquired from the whole congregation in his own way.

"I would like to go back to the Arab era."

Arsalan, who is keen on camels, food and desert, said he was happy.

"And Hamza you?"

"During the rule of Mamun al-Rashid, when they gave the British a watch as a gift, they considered the crocodile to be the magic of the Muslims. I would like to tell them that today, We are proud of our inventions. Science was developed because of our forefathers. "

The whole group had expressed their views, some wanted to meet their favorite poet, some wanted to go back to the Mughal era, of all the children, only Haider wanted to go to his future.

"Time travel, by the way, is considered by many to be a mental idea, but they do not think that it is mentioned in our religion of Islam. There are some references to it in the Quran as well. " The virtue of Sir Ibad was that he taught science with the argument of religion.
The event of Ascension is a clear example of the time journey that every believer believes in, the journey from Makkah to Jerusalem at this hour of the night and then from there onwards to Sidra Al-Muntaha (Subhan Allah). And back in the afternoon, while the door latch was still shaking and the bed was warm. " (Surah Asra)
Only Sir Ibad's voice was echoing in the congregation.

Science is also proving today that when the velocity is equal to the speed of light, then according to the theory of relativity, time travels at the speed of light stops our age. I have, when he slept for probably three hundred years, his few hours of sleep spanned years.

One thing that is common between Surah Al-Kahf and Fitna Dajjal is that time travel seems to be common to both "time and space" ie "time and space". In all the information we have about the Antichrist, time and space theory has been found. The first day of the Antichrist will be equal to one year, that is, the speed of time will decrease.

The people who seem to be talking about theories and the time machine today are fourteen hundred years old.

Our religion, Islam, is the most modern religion. I wish we could understand the verses of the Qur'an and try to find out. This book is a book of secrets between the believers and Allah. "

The hour of the parade was over. As soon as they left, Hamza and Haider started planning to make a time machine together.

Short story by Javeria Aziz

<u>BIO:</u> *Javeria Aziz is a creative story writer belongs to Pakistan. She is a creative writer who thought to change society through her stories and convey meaningful message to her readers. she create the dialogue, the characters and the storyline of a script, a sci-fiction , fantasy, thriller suspense and romance author.*

Follow @anonymousoul23